DODD, MEAD WONDERS BOOKS

Wonders of Caribou

JIM REARDEN

Illustrated with photographs by the author

DODD, MEAD & COMPANY
New York

PICTURE CREDITS

Photographs courtesy of the U.S. Fish and Wildlife Service, Robert D. Jones, Jr., page 14; John M. Kauffmann, page 17. All other photographs are by the author.

The map on page 6 is by Donald T. Pitcher.

Library of Congress Cataloging in Publication Data

Rearden, Jim.
Wonders of caribou.

Bibliography: p.
Includes index.
SUMMARY: Discusses the physical character-
istics, behavior, migratory habits, and the relationship
to man of the North American caribou.
1. Caribou—Juvenile literature. [1. Caribou]
I. Title.
QL737.U55R42   599'.7357   76-12512
ISBN 0-396-07361-1

Contents

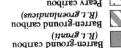

Barren-ground caribou
(*R. t. granti*)

Barren-ground caribou
(*R. t. groenlandicus*)

Peary caribou
(*R.t. pearyi*)

Woodland caribou
(*R.t. caribou*)

 Trans-Alaska pipeline (under construction)

The Range of
CARIBOU
in North America

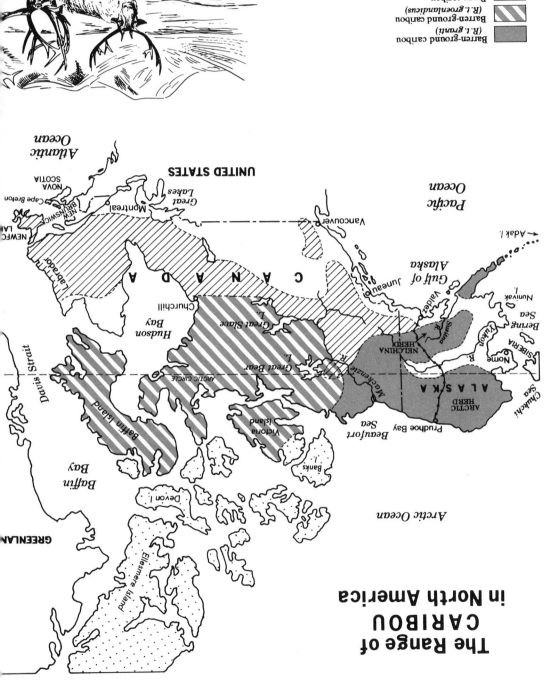

Atlantic Ocean

UNITED STATES

NOVA SCOTIA

Cape Breton

NEW BRUNSWICK

NEWFC

Great Lakes

Montreal

Labrador

C A N A D A

Churchill

Hudson Bay

Great Slave L.

Great Bear L.

Mackenzie R.

ARCTIC CIRCLE

Pacific Ocean

Vancouver

Juneau

Gulf of Alaska

Valdez

Adak I.

Nunivak I.

Bering Sea

Yukon R.

Nome

SIBERIA

Chukchi Sea

A L A S K A

ARCTIC HERD

NELCHINA HERD

Prudhoe Bay

Beaufort Sea

Victoria Island

Banks I.

Devon I.

Baffin Island

Baffin Bay

Davis Strait

GREENLAN

Ellesmere Island

Arctic Ocean

1

Where Caribou Are Found

Caribou are the most abundant large mammals in northern Alaska and northern Canada, sometimes found in vast herds that number in the hundreds of thousands. They have ranged the *tundra* (treeless plains of the North) and *taiga* (swampy, coniferous, northern forest) of the Northern Hemisphere for more than a million years. At one time caribou were abundant in North America as far south as the mountains of New Mexico.

Climate changes and the northern advance of man and his civilization have restricted the caribou's distribution. Today Canada and Alaska have most of the world's wild caribou, although there are perhaps 30,000 wild caribou, or reindeer, in Norway, Sweden, and Finland. Another 100,000 are found on the Taimyr Peninsula in Siberia.

Caribou in Alaska and Canada

Alaska has thirteen herds of barren-ground caribou (*Rangifer tarandus granti*). Ten of these are found entirely within the state, and three wander from Alaska into Canada and back. Altogether, there are about 260,000 caribou in Alaska. The two largest herds, in northern Alaska, consist of about 100,000 animals each.

Canada has four major populations of a closely related barren-ground caribou (*Rangifer tarandus groenlandicus*), named for

7

the regions they inhabit—Bluenose, Bathurst, Beverly, and Kaminuriak. They total about half a million; at one time there were probably two or three million.

In addition, on the islands of far northern Canada is the small Peary caribou (*Rangifer tarandus pearyi*), numbering only about 25,000.

The woodland caribou of Canada (*Rangifer tarandus caribou*) is a creature of the forests, which usually seeks the seclusion of mature spruce and other coniferous forests, or remote alpine meadows. These caribou are not as restless as their brothers of the tundra, for they travel little.

Woodland caribou of Canada have decreased greatly. For example, the 10,000 animals now found on the island of Newfoundland are but a fraction of the number estimated fifty years ago. They are gone from Nova Scotia, New Brunswick, and some other areas of their former range, and have been reintroduced to Cape Breton Island.

Past over-hunting in some areas and changes in habitat in others brought about the decline. Clearing of land for agriculture has destroyed habitat for caribou. Vast areas of forest have been logged or burned, and replaced by new growth which is much more suitable for moose and deer than for caribou. Although caribou eat grasses and sedges, they depend heavily upon *lichens*, which require many years to mature before being useful to them. Lichens are slow-growing plant forms, a fungus and an alga living together. There are many forms of lichen, but barren-ground caribou mostly use those of the genus *Cladonia*, a ground-dwelling form, while woodland caribou eat tree-growing lichens.

Prevention of forest fires and closed or strictly limited hunting seasons have brought a recent increase in Canada's woodland caribou, and hunting these animals is now permitted over most of their range.

No caribou are considered endangered in North America, although where the woodland caribou extends its range, where a few animals live at the edge of the natural range in the Northern Great Lakes states, special attention must be paid or minor habitat changes or hunting could easily eliminate them in the United States.

The Caribou's Home

The northern Canada and Alaska home of wild caribou is mostly unsettled, with few villages or cities. There are no fences and few roads. This is a rugged land, with long, extremely cold winters and short summers. During winter the ground is covered with snow, and lakes and streams are frozen over. Temperatures often plunge to $-50°$ F., or colder.

Winter days in this region are short, lasting only a few hours in December. In the extreme northern part of the caribou's range, the sun does not rise above the horizon for several months during winter, and light from the sun provides only a dim glow for a short time each day. The brightness of the snow insures that there is a certain amount of light available except on the darkest of cloudy nights.

On the other hand, during summer it is light almost twenty-four hours a day over much of the range of the caribou. The long hours of sunlight hasten the melting of snow from the previous winter, and in spring and summer plants grow rapidly.

Much of the land is underlain with *permafrost*—permanently frozen ground. Above the permafrost is a layer of ground called the "active layer," which thaws during warm summer months and in which plants grow.

Permafrost forms a layer that is impenetrable to water, and meltwater from snow, as well as rainwater, lies on top of the ground. As a result, much of the ground is soggy, and there are hundreds of thousands of ponds and lakes.

9

A team of sled-pulling reindeer. One of these animals has shed both antlers; the other retains one.

REINDEER

In Russia, Norway, Sweden, and Finland, the animal we call "caribou" is called "reindeer." Few wild reindeer are left in the world, but many are raised as domestic animals. They are herded by their owners and, like other animals man has domesticated, provide meat, hides, and even milk, to their owners. Reindeer are used for pulling sleds, and larger ones are ridden.

This wet land is ideal for mosquitoes and black flies, which depend upon water for their life cycles. These insects are serious pests to all warm-blooded animals that live in the Far North. When insects are most numerous, usually in July and August, caribou often climb high hills or mountains, seeking breezes. Sometimes caribou plunge into lakes or even into the Arctic Ocean, to escape these buzzing and biting pests.

Between 1891 and 1902, 1,280 Siberian reindeer (*Rangifer tarandus tarandus*) were moved to Alaska. These increased until, by the 1930s, there were more than 600,000 reindeer in Alaska, all owned by their herders. Most of these animals were kept in a 100-mile-wide strip along the coast of western Alaska where it faces the Bering and Chukchi seas.

Canada bought a herd of these reindeer, and they were driven across Alaska to the Mackenzie River delta in Canada. Their descendants are still being herded by Eskimos.

In Alaska, many reindeer starved because there were too many for the amount of food or pasture. Wolves became abundant and killed many. Herds of roaming caribou swept away other reindeer, which went wild and remained with the wandering caribou.

A mature bull reindeer. Closely related to caribou, some reindeer are hard to tell from their wild cousins.

Today there are about 30,000 reindeer under man's control in different herds in Alaska. Canada has about 3,000 reindeer, all on the Mackenzie River delta.

Alaska's and Canada's reindeer are shorter legged than wild caribou; the type of reindeer brought to Alaska from Siberia had short legs. Some Old World strains of reindeer are much larger, and have longer legs. The reindeer in Alaska and Canada are sometimes spotted or white. Wild caribou are never spotted, and they are rarely white, except for the Peary caribou of northern Canada, which may approach white.

Reindeer introduced to America from Siberia and America's wild caribou interbreed freely. In an attempt to increase the size of reindeer on Nunivak Island, which lies in the Bering Sea off Alaska's coast, bull caribou were released on the island. As a result of interbreeding with caribou, the reindeer of Nunivak Island became larger than other Alaskan reindeer—but they also became wilder, and more difficult to herd and handle.

Possibly as recently as 20,000 years ago, ancestors of North America's caribou and of Europe's reindeer roamed freely between Alaska and Siberia on the land bridge between Siberia and Alaska.

2

Physical Characteristics

The caribou is a member of the deer family, or Cervidae, of which there are approximately 100 species throughout the world. A few of the others in the family are the white-tailed deer of the eastern and southern United States, the black-tailed and mule deer of the West, the elk, and moose.

All members of the family are even-toed, have hooves, and have a stomach which includes four compartments. They lack upper front teeth and shed their antlers annually. Antlers are not to be confused with horns, which are permanent growths and not shed.

SIZE AND GROWTH

Caribou are moderate- to large-sized deer. Bulls do not reach full size until they are at least six years old, cows at least three. In southcentral Alaska, an average, full-grown, barren-ground bull measures about 50 inches high at the shoulders and weighs about 400 pounds. A full-grown cow is about 43 inches high at the shoulders and weighs about 220 pounds.

There is much variation among individuals and over the range of the caribou. Scientists have learned, however, that caribou become larger where there is abundant feed and a longer plant growing season. Caribou that live in the Arctic, where the growing season is short, are generally smaller than animals that live in sub-Arctic regions.

Proof of the role of food and climate on the ultimate size of caribou came when twenty-three caribou calves were moved from the Nelchina herd in southcentral Alaska to Adak Island in the Aleutian Island chain. Adak is about 750 miles south, 1,400 miles southwest, of the original home of these animals. Here, with a longer growing season and milder winters, the animals became much larger. Full-grown bull caribou at Adak Island now weigh nearly 700 pounds, which is about 300 pounds more than the average weight of the bulls found in the Nelchina herd where they originated.

The growth of young caribou largely ceases during most of the winter, a protective trait of the animals. This period of growth dormancy from October through February occurs ir-

These animals were released on Adak Island to build up a herd.

respective of food supply, and appears to be caused by the shorter daylight hours. Even replacement growth of teeth probably stops during these months. When spring and summer return with an abundance of easily obtained food, the growth of the young animals resumes.

ANTLERS

The most striking physical trait of the caribou is its antlers. The huge, graceful, and many pointed antlers of a mature bull caribou are among the most spectacular of any of the deer. Trophy-hunting sportsmen value these great antlers, and travel great distances in order to collect them.

The caribou is the only member of the deer family in which both the male and female have antlers. Even the calves grow antlers, starting with tiny buttons that emerge a month after birth. By the time a calf is four months old, it carries prominent spikes. When calves are six months old, males have spikes about ten inches long, while the females have spikes that are about six inches long.

Antlers are shed and regrown each year. They are used for defense against predators, and they are also important to cows in

A sportsman with a fine Alaskan caribou

winter, when it is important for these mothers-to-be to have the choicest foods. Cows, which carry hard antlers through the winter, can prod even large old bulls away from favored feeding sites, for the bulls shed their antlers and are bald-headed through the winter months.

Squabbling within the herd that erupts into fights usually results in "boxing," with forefeet, rather than fights with antlers. Most antler fighting between caribou occurs between bulls during breeding season, but is seldom long or drawn out. A few quick contacts, a clatter of antler against antler, and caribou bulls usually break apart and the battle is over.

Some people erroneously believe that caribou use their antlers to dig through the snow for food. Caribou use their front feet for digging, not their antlers.

Antlers of an adult bull caribou are composed of two heavy main *beams*, each leading back from the forehead, then sweeping upward about halfway and curving forward near the tip. A pair of *brow tines* extends directly forward from the base of the antlers, and either one or both of these may be flattened into a broad vertical *shovel*, which often extends nearly to the nose. Above the brow tines and growing forward is a pair of even longer tines, known as the *bez-tines*. These have few points, and even occasionally are a single spike.

There are many variations of antlers, and no two ever seem to be exactly the same. The striking feature of the mature bull's antlers is their size in relation to the animal's body. The average length of the antler beam of adult bulls is greater than the average shoulder height of the bulls. Some beams measure as much as sixty inches long, along the curve, from base to tip. Beam shape of caribou antlers varies greatly. Some animals have mostly rounded beams. Others have flat beams. Most are flattened at least toward the tips.

The antlers of the cow are small replicas of those of the bull.

16

The brow tine is often only a round prong, or modified into a shovel much smaller than that of the male. There is a tendency toward few points. One to three percent of cows never grow antlers.

Young bulls have antlers that are similar to those of the cow until the animals are two or three years old. When a bull is three, his antlers become more massive, more complex, with more points and with a clearly developed shovel. They are then easily distinguishable from the antlers of cows.

By March bulls that are six years old or older start to grow new antlers. Antlers for younger bulls start growing a little later. Growing antlers are covered with *velvet*, which is the term used to describe the velvety-appearing, fine-haired skin covering developing antlers. This skin is rich in blood vessels which carry nutrients to the fast-growing antlers.

After May, antlers of the bulls grow very rapidly, so that by July adult bulls have antlers that are two or three feet long.

Five young caribou

They are heavy and cumbersome looking because of the thick velvet.

By August the bulls' antlers have reached full length. At this time the velvet starts to drop off, and the bulls seek small trees and bushes to rub their antlers on. Rubbing removes the shreds of velvet, and polishes the hardening beams and spikes.

During the September-October breeding season, the bulls' straw-colored antlers are clean and polished and seem to flash in the sunlight, especially against a dark background. At this time the cows' antlers are still largely covered with velvet, as their growth is about six months out of phase with that of the bulls.

By early November, the bulls shed their antlers, the oldest animals first. By February all bulls, with the exception of year-lings and a few two-year-olds, have lost their antlers. The bald-headed animals are strikingly different in appearance from when they carry full-grown antlers.

Cows lose the velvet during late October, and carry antlers until April or May. Pregnant cows usually retain their antlers until their calves are born in late May, and then shed them within a few days. Other cows lose antlers from April to June, with the oldest cows shedding earliest. New antlers develop in the velvet during summer and early fall.

Antlers of the bull, as they are regrown each year, increase in length and massiveness annually, until they are the largest when the bull is between six and nine years old. After that, antlers become smaller, as the animal enters old age. Antlers of the cow change little in size after the animal is two years old.

HAIR

The *pelage*, or hair, of caribou is dense and long when compared with that of other deer. Two types of hair found on these animals are long *guard hairs*, which make up most of the hair, and dense *underwool*. The underwool is hidden by the guard

New fresh coats and velvet-covered antlers of caribou in August give the animals a handsome look.

hairs and lies close to the skin.

The guard hairs are enlarged toward the tips to form a tight coat during winter when the hair is longest. Added insulation is provided by large empty cells found in the guard hairs. Even the ears and tail of caribou are well furred, and the muzzle is completely covered with hair.

The legs of caribou generally have shorter hair than the rest of the body. This could result in much loss of heat in extreme cold. However, scientists have discovered that during winter the caribou's legs are maintained at a cooler temperature than the rest of the body. Thus the animal lives with cold legs and feet all winter. This saves much heat. Conversely, in warmer seasons, when too much heat may be a problem for a caribou, as when it is fleeing from wolves and gets too warm, the legs are probably the main area of the body where it releases extra heat.

Each summer all of the hairs of a caribou are shed, or molted, as new hairs grow in. The new hairs continue to grow, and by winter they form an exceedingly thick, long coat. By late winter and spring the caribou's coat has become badly worn. The hair becomes brittle and the brown tips break off the guard hairs easily, and the grayish-white bases of the hair show. As a result all caribou become much lighter in color at this time of year.

There also may be some bleaching from the longer daylight hours, with the sun reflecting from snow. By late spring most caribou appear whitish.

In May large patches of hair are often missing—worn off by the animal's bedding habits. In some cases the hair may become frozen to the thawing ice- and snow-covered ground where the animal lies down, and the hair remains stuck to the ground as the animal stands up.

Caribou are at their handsomest in September and October when they have new coats, new antlers, and are fat from abundant summer feed. The *mane* that grows on the bottom side of the neck of old bulls is snowy white, and the neck is also white. Seen from a distance, the white neck and the great straw-colored antlers are particularly striking. Other parts of the caribou bull at this time of year are clove brown, with a whitish band along the middle of the sides. The belly is also largely white.

The new coat of the adult cow is generally like that of the bull, but it isn't as striking. Instead of white on the neck, the cow is grayish-white, and has hardly any ventral mane on the neck. The yearling caribou is very dark in its new fall coat. The hair is a rich dark seal-brown, with few light colored patches.

TEETH

The caribou has small teeth, for it is a dainty feeder. The teeth are well adapted to the soft, fine plant parts the animal eats. There are no upper incisors, or front teeth, but the upper jaw has a hard pad against which the lower incisors are clamped when the animal nips plants. The lower incisors are loosely set in their sockets so they are flexible.

As with other mammals, the caribou calf is born with temporary or baby teeth. As the calf grows, these teeth are shed, to be replaced with permanent teeth. All thirty-four permanent teeth grow in by the time the animal is about twenty-five months old.

THE STOMACH

In eating, the caribou nips tiny leaves, grass, and twigs, mushrooms, and other plant materials, and immediately swallows them. The food descends through the esophagus, where it goes mostly to the *rumen*, the first and largest of the four stomach compartments. Some of the finer food parts, however, may go into the *reticulem*, which is the second compartment.

While in the rumen, leaves, twigs, and other food are mixed, kneaded, and churned by muscular action. Enzymes present in the rumen commence breaking down the fibers.

After feeding, the caribou likes to find a pleasant place to lie down and ruminate. The food it has swallowed has started to ferment and break down. At intervals, a small portion of the contents of the rumen, called a *bolus*, is returned to the mouth for chewing. This is done with the molars, which have a shearing action as the lower jaw is moved sideways.

After chewing, the caribou swallows the material again, and the finer parts are moved on into the other three compartments of the stomach: the reticulem, the *omasum*, and *abomasum*.

The rumen and reticulem are constantly filled with liquid. As food particles move into the other stomach parts, there is less and less liquid. The broken-down vegetation that finally leaves the stomach is fluid or semifluid, and is called *chyme*. The

Caribou ruminating after feeding

chyme moves on into the small intestine where it is digested. The digestive process associated with the rumen produces much heat, which helps the caribou to maintain its body temperature during cold weather.

HOOVES

Caribou hooves are very well adapted to the northern environment. They are very broad, and the two main toes of the cloven hoof are well developed. The *dewclaws* help support a caribou's weight, important in loose snow and in swampy areas. The dewclaws on most other deer are relatively unimportant in helping to support the animal's weight. Another species of deer generally found in the Far North, the moose, combats deep snow and summer swamps with long legs. The lighter weight caribou depends upon his huge hooves to carry him across on top. Essentially, the caribou carries his own snowshoes.

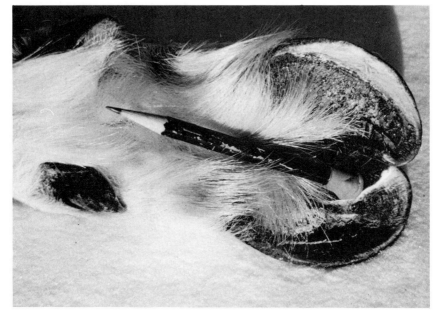

The sharp, horny underside of a caribou's hoof

Caribou running on glare ice

In winter the edges of caribou hooves grow long and the foot-pad underneath shrinks and becomes hard and horny. Long bristlelike hairs, which grow thickly during winter, surround the hoof and form tufts which cover the fleshy pad on the underside.

During winter, caribou walk on the thin, crescent-shaped, horny rim of the hoof. This allows them to walk easily on slippery ice. Caribou can cross hard-crusted snow almost without leaving a track.

Caribou feeding in packed or crusted snow chop into the hard snow with their sharp front hooves, as they dig down two feet or more to reach plants they need for food.

In loose snow the big hooves are helpful in tossing large amounts of snow behind, as the animals dig to reach food.

The sharp, broad hooves are important in the survival of caribou when they flee from their principal enemy, the wolf, for they allow the agile animals to climb into steep rocky areas and cross hard snow banks and icy surfaces swiftly and safely.

23

3

Caribou Migrations

"No one knows the ways of the wind or the caribou," Indians of northern Canada say. There is much truth in the statement, for the barren-ground caribou wanders all of its life, and never remains in one area for very long. Within a year's time, a caribou herd usually migrates from summer to winter range, and back to the summer area. Small herds of caribou apparently migrate less than large herds. The Nelchina herd in Alaska migrated a distance of 370 miles in 1955, when the small herd of about 10,000 was growing. In 1964, when the herd had grown to more than 60,000 animals, it migrated 980 miles during a year.

The vast migrations of huge herds of caribou have been recorded by explorers, traders, trappers, and hunters. Many have reported watching a "sea" of caribou moving by. After a time it seems to the observers that the caribou are standing still, and the hill they stand upon is moving through the massed animals. The noises of clattering antlers, grunting caribou, and the clicking of hooves make a low, muffled roar.

Caribou migrations are unpredictable. Since the animals move such a great distance, it is difficult to keep track of them over a large area. Sometimes the animals seemingly disappear. Sometimes they scatter over an area so thinly that it is very difficult to find any caribou, even when searching with an airplane.

A traveling band of caribou cows and young calves passing across a snowdrift in late May

At other times they flock together into compact herds of thousands.

Stragglers may be seen in caribou country at almost any time of the year. Yet an area that is known for many years to have great numbers of caribou may suddenly be abandoned, as the animals change their migratory routes.

CARIBOU LOCOMOTION

Caribou are marvelous travelers. They can move great distances swiftly and easily, using a variety of gaits. These various gaits can, without difficulty, carry the animals forty miles in one day across mountain and tundra.

A gallop is the caribou's fastest pace. One scientist clocked a group of adult bull caribou at thirty-eight miles an hour on a road with hard-packed snow. Another clocked a young bull at thirty-seven miles an hour as it galloped on a frozen lake. The gallop is tiring to a caribou, however, and it can maintain this gait for only a few miles at most.

25

A trot is commonly used by caribou in covering ground rapidly. Note that the right-rear and left-front hooves are off the ground at the same time.

For long-distance travel when in a hurry, a caribou trots. The head is held high and forelegs lift and reach with each step. Most of the up-and-down movement is with the legs, and the caribou's back glides along smoothly. Caribou can travel up to about twenty-five miles an hour at a trot. With this gait they can cross hummocky, rough ground smoothly and with seeming ease. No other northern mammal can travel across rough ground so easily.

For long-distance travel, caribou mostly use a fast walk. The fast walk of a caribou is much faster than that of a man. Indeed a man has to jog rapidly to keep up with a walking caribou.

The same migration routes tend to be used year after year, the same mountain passes, and the same river crossings. Because caribou commonly travel single file, deep trails are worn into the ground. These trails are found wherever there are caribou in any numbers in Alaska and Canada. Such trails average about ten to twelve inches wide, and they may be six inches deep.

The habit of caribou *trailing*, or traveling single file, has importance to the caribou and other creatures of the North. By traveling in this manner, caribou reduce the amount of trampling of valuable food plants by sharp hooves. Other animals, including man, follow caribou trails, finding it makes walking easier. Caribou trails are conspicuous features of the land throughout the North. They follow around mountains, around ridges, and across valleys; many such trails often parallel one another.

Caribou are strong swimmers. Helped by their broad hooves, which are excellent paddles, they commonly plunge into water without hesitation. This is a necessity, for they must cross many lakes and rivers on their long-distance treks. In the water they float higher than most mammals, with their heads and backs well above waterline, held up by their abundant, buoyant hair.

Even calves take to the water when very young, usually swimming downstream of their mothers. However, sometimes when large rivers are high and herds of cows with young calves cross them, many calves are drowned. Once the cows of Alaska's Nelchina herd crossed the Susitna River at high water four times almost immediately after calving. Many calves were drowned.

Caribou commonly travel single file. These cows are climbing a steep snowdrift.

Fall and Spring Migrations

In late August or early September, caribou herds begin a leisurely drift toward winter ranges, which may be from 50 to 500 miles or more away. Breeding takes place on the way, and the animals then hurry on to wintering areas, where they scatter widely in small bands.

In late winter, scattered pregnant cows and their yearlings, or calves from the previous year, start gathering. Small herds are formed, then sometimes larger and larger herds. Between mid-March and April they start traveling on their spring migration to calving grounds. Some herds travel as much as 500 miles to reach calving areas. At first the migration is slow, but as the May and early June time of calving comes near, the animals move faster and faster.

At this time of year the attachment between the mothers and their yearlings breaks down, and the yearlings start to gather in small herds of their own. They commonly intermingle with the migrating older cows.

The bulls, both young and old, also migrate toward the calving area, but they move more slowly. Some males never reach the calving grounds.

Weather can change the timing of spring migration. An early spring, when the snow melts quickly, may cause caribou to move to the calving grounds early. But late, lingering snows may delay the migration as much as a month. At times the animals may not reach the calving area, and calves may be born on the way.

After reaching the calving area, cows scatter widely. In northern Canada and Arctic Alaska, calves generally arrive between June first and fifth. In southcentral Alaska, calving commences during the second week of May.

About two weeks after calving, cows and their new calves form increasingly large groups, and remain in such groups until early August. Bulls and yearlings may also form into large

A band of yearlings crossing an open hillside in late spring

bands, but they usually remain separate from the cows throughout the summer.

WHY CARIBOU MIGRATE

Caribou migrate probably because of a need for food. Scientists have noted that caribou herds of less than about 10,000 move relatively short distances. But when a herd grows larger, it starts to migrate farther each year. Caribou may have an inborn trait that causes them to become restless when their numbers increase, causing them to move farther and farther in their search for food.

When caribou are abundant in an area, the best food is quickly nipped and eaten, and the animals *must* move on to find the choice morsels they like. Migrating, then, may be a self-regulating mechanism of the species, which helps the caribou to survive. It has obvious advantages in spreading the pressure of grazing over a larger area, which is to the benefit of the caribou as a race.

4

Food and Feeding Habits

Caribou live from the permanent snow fields high in the mountains to the dense spruce forests of the river valleys. They wander to the sea itself, and roam across vast tundra regions. In this extraordinary range of habitat, caribou find and eat a great variety of plants. This is an important adaptation to living in the North, where soil is often poor and plant growth small.

The metabolism of many northern *ungulates*, or hooved plant-eaters, slows in winter, and this holds true with caribou. A caribou's body demands less food during the winter months, and, as mentioned earlier, its growth ceases, regardless of the amount of food available.

Shortening daylight hours seem to trigger the caribou's slower rate of metabolism. Low heat loss from the body because of the new heavy coat, lack of breeding activity, hair and antler growth, and fly harassment combine to keep total expenditure of energy to a minimum. Further, the caribou can move about easily on snow and ice with their huge, sharp-edged hooves, and normally can easily dig or chop through snow to get food. In fact, caribou are so well adapted, there is less physiological strain on them in winter than at any other time of year.

Nonetheless, snow conditions are important to the caribou. When an ice crust forms on top of the snow—which may happen with a winter rain, or when it suddenly warms, only to turn bitterly cold again—caribou may be unable to chop through the ice that is formed to get food. Some caribou starve as a result; many times they will move to seek better conditions.

Winter

In early winter, caribou feed on sedge around the shores of lakes and in bogs. Herds of caribou in the sub-Arctic, where there are open stands of spruce trees, like to spend much time at lower elevations in these stands, especially on flat muskeg areas where there are many lakes, ponds, and bogs. These wet areas are frozen over, of course, but often the green plants that grow around them can be reached by pawing through the snow.

When feeding, the caribou sniffs the top of the snow. When it smells plants it wants to eat, it paws through the snow with its

An aerial photograph of a group of caribou that have fed out of spruce timber into an open, snow-covered meadow.

front hooves, at times lowering its nose to sniff into the hole. It digs with alternate swipes and pawings of the forefeet, tossing snow behind, until the food is exposed. Where snow is shallow and loose, the caribou just pushes the snow aside with its furry muzzle.

An area where a herd of caribou has fed through the snow looks as if it has been dug by hundreds of men with shovels, and holes where caribou have pawed for food are called *craters*. Animals may quarrel over digging spots, and old and cranky cows with antlers may prod in the rear or the side of big, antler-less bulls, forcing them to move so the cows can dig in the favored spot.

Another source of green food plants for caribou in winter in lake and pond areas is that of muskrat *push-ups*. The muskrat, a

A caribou, chest deep in loose snow

small, water-living rodent, commonly cuts green water plants and carries them to the surface of the lake or pond where it lives. It uses the greens to surround breathing holes in the ice. These push-ups can be recognized easily as the small mounds under the snow on lakes wherever muskrats are found.

Caribou paw through the snow to these push-ups and eat the green plant material. This probably means death to the muskrat, that depends upon the push-ups to keep his breathing hole in the ice open.

Often caribou return to higher elevations after about November, where they dig sedges and lichens. In deep snow areas, wind-blown ridgetops generally have little or no snow, making it easier to reach food plants.

Lichens, which may take as long as thirty-five years to mature, become increasingly important to caribou as winter progresses, and no other ungulate seems as well adapted to eating them. They are very acidic and relatively low in food value. Yet where caribou are abundant, these favored plants are often eaten until there are none left, forcing the animals to seek other foods.

SPRING

Spring is the most critical time for caribou, for they are recovering from the long winter and starting to regrow antlers and new coats. Most caribou cows migrate hundreds of miles to the calving grounds during the month or so before giving birth. Such a long trek requires much energy, and the cows are in poor condition when they arrive. They need the new plant growth of spring badly, which helps them produce abundant, rich milk for the calves and recover from the strains of their travels.

Caribou calves get their early meals almost on the run, for they nurse briefly and frequently. One scientist timed the length of 143 nursings—they averaged 32 seconds each.

Sometimes spring is late, and winter snows are slow in melt-

33

An hours-old calf rests and watches as its mother feeds. Notice the large feet on this cow.

ing. When this occurs, caribou cows have difficulty in obtaining the food they need for themselves and their calves. As a result, calves in such years may be smaller than normal. Small calves do not survive as well as do larger ones, and mortality of caribou calves is much higher during a late-arriving spring.

From mid-April to mid-June, the new growth of grasses and sedges is important caribou food, as are the leaves and buds of certain willows—which are bushes, not trees, in the Far North—and of dwarf birch, a plant that seldom grows more than knee-high.

A large number of other juicy plants are eaten as they start to grow in the long daylight hours. Lichens are incidental foods to

A tranquil bunch of caribou cows feeding with their week-old calves in a sheltered valley in Alaska

caribou at this time of year, unless snow lies on the ground later than usual.

SUMMER

During summer, mid-June to mid-August, caribou have available a wide variety of plants. Basic foods remain the soft moist parts of leaves, buds, stem tips of willows, dwarf birch, grasses, and sedges, but a large number of other soft-stemmed plants are also used. Mushrooms are a favorite in late summer. If caribou can find enough mushrooms, they feed on them almost entirely.

Caribou eat as they walk, nipping plants here and there, preferring only the finer parts, such as smaller leaves, buds, and stem tips. Caribou browsing on dwarf birch and willow grasp the branches in their mouths, draw their heads backward and upward, and scrape off the leaves and small buds and tips between their lower incisor teeth and the horny palate of the upper jaw. The reaching and lifting of caribou heads produces a head-bobbing pattern characteristic of the animals at this time of year.

Summer is a time of great energy demands on caribou. Cows are still nursing calves, which now graze and are growing rapidly. Bulls and cows are growing their huge antlers. All caribou are shedding and growing an entirely new coat of hair and are laying on fat stores for fall and winter.

FALL

During fall, mid-August to mid-October, caribou shift their selection of food to winter forage plants as the cold freezes and withers summer foods. They eat green plants that remain in moist sites. And they move to lower elevations at this time of year as winter nears. Lichens become more important to them for food, but they still prefer mushrooms as long as they are available. They like to feed on green sedges around lakes, ponds, and bogs. Browse plants—willow and dwarf birch— become less important.

By September the calves are suckling only occasionally. When the first heavy snows fall in October, the five-month-old calves have no difficulty in finding food and pawing aside the snow. They are weaned between September and December.

During the breeding season in late September and October, adult bull caribou eat very little, if at all. They are busy seeking cows, and driving younger bulls away from the cows they find. Before breeding season, the bulls are fat and sleek, and most of them have stored a twenty- to thirty-pound pad of fat over their rump and back. They live largely off this stored fat during the *rut*, or reproductive period, which lasts about three weeks. Most breeding bulls then start the winter in their poorest condition of the year. This is generally unimportant to the race, for the bulls have served their main function in breeding the cows.

5

Caribou Behavior

GENERAL TRAITS

At all seasons the barren-ground caribou is gregarious and is usually found in small bands or loose herds. The herd is a social group, consisting of different ages and sexes at different times of the year. There is no recognizable leader, although an old cow is more frequently seen as the lead animal in a traveling group. Individual animals shift easily from one band or herd to another.

Caribou are rather easily approached by man, and they often appear to be somewhat stupid. This may be because in a herd there is a tendency for each to depend on others for detecting danger. The individual caribou is so accustomed to hearing sounds made by other caribou that it may ignore the snapping of twigs or other noises made by man, wolves, or other possible enemies.

Caribou have good eyesight. When animals are nervous and wary, especially a cow with a newborn calf, a lone caribou, or animals in a small group, the sight of a human head peering from behind a tree or a rock from as much as 400 yards' distance may alarm them. Yet often when caribou see a strange object, they seem unable to understand that it may be dangerous. Often they stand and stare. Usually after staring for a time, they resort

Curious yearling caribou approach a photographer, then turn and flee. They may return for another look.

to their most important sense, that of smell, and move downwind of the object.

One can often stand in plain view of caribou and watch as they retreat in panic, only to advance, and edge around to get downwind to try your scent. Sometimes when a caribou, muzzle extended, tests the wind current carrying scent from man, it leaps with fright and runs away. Other times, the curious animal may return again and again to sample what may be a strange new odor.

One oddity of the caribou is its habit of sometimes lapsing into a deep, sound sleep. Occasionally a man can walk up to and touch such a sleeping caribou. An Alaskan hunter named Frank Glaser once leaped on a sleeping caribou, held it down while it struggled, and got its legs tied. Then he took it to a nearby barn, where it soon became tame and learned to pull a sled.

Caribou are usually silent, but at times they communicate with one another with a piglike grunt. Cows call their calves with a grunt, and a calf apparently recognizes the sound of its mother. A scientist watching a group of cows and calves scattered over a wide area heard a cow grunt. Only one calf responded—hers. It ran directly to its mother, while other calves ignored the sound.

Calves bawl frequently during their first few months of life, and adults may snort loudly when annoyed by insects or surprised by man or a wolf at close range.

HEAD BOBBING

Within moments of its birth a caribou calf knows what its mother wants when she stands in front of it and bobs her head up and down. The message to the calf is for it to follow her. This is but one of the many signals used by caribou in communicating with one another.

Caribou may also bob their heads when they come to a cliff or a deep river which looks dangerous. After bobbing their heads, caribou usually turn and seek a safe way down a steep bank, or seek a shallow, less swift place to cross a dangerous river.

Caribou that are alarmed or suspicious of a strange or unusual object may also bob their heads. Occasionally when adult caribou meet, head bobbing may take place.

ALARM POSE

When a caribou sees at a distance a wolf, man, or any object that is frightening, it may assume the *alarm pose*. The alarm pose consists of head up, ears standing high and pointed forward, tail raised, and one hind leg extended out to one side.

Other caribou seeing an animal in the alarm pose immediately turn to look at whatever the first has seen. Occasionally the caribou giving the alarm grunts as it assumes the pose, especially

The alarm pose (left two caribou) indicates that these caribou see something unusual, or something that worries them.

if it is a cow with a calf.

If the animal that has assumed the alarm pose then runs, this causes other caribou to flee, even though they may not have seen whatever it was that caused the alarm.

EXCITATION LEAP

Another significant means of communication is the *excitation leap*. This "spy hop," as one scientist called it, is usually performed by a bull, although almost any age or sex of caribou may do it. It occurs usually when something suddenly surprises and frightens a caribou—a wolf dashing into sight or a man suddenly appearing close by. The frightened caribou suddenly raises itself high on its hind legs, sometimes actually running a few feet before the front legs touch the ground again. The caribou then continues to gallop away from whatever it was that frightened or surprised it. Other caribou seeing a herd member perform an excitation leap get the message that there is something to fear, and they, too, gallop off at full speed.

But this isn't all there is to the excitation leap. As the animal that performs the leap puts its entire weight on the hind feet, the cloven hooves spread, and an alarm scent is left on the ground with each step.

Caribou coming to a place where an animal has made an excitation leap—even hours later, when the frightened animal is long out of sight—smell the alarm scent, and they too take alarm and flee the area.

Even caribou that are not alarmed leave some scent to mark where they have passed. Eskimo hunters have long known that if the leading animals of a caribou migration are allowed to pass unmolested, the rest of the herd will follow. If, on the other hand, some excited hunter frightens the leaders in a migration by shooting, and they turn back, the rest of the herd which follows hours or days later may also turn back.

6

The Caribou Calf

Long-legged, reddish-brown caribou calves are born approximately 225 to 235 days after the late September, early October breeding season. Calves generally remain with their mothers through the fall and winter. When the herd starts to migrate toward calving grounds in early April, many of the short-yearlings (calves that are less than one year old) are left or driven off by their mothers. After that they are on their own.

Although other members of the deer family commonly bear twins, caribou have a single calf—an adaptation to a wandering life.

WEIGHT

At birth the average weight of caribou calves is thirteen pounds. Some may weigh as little as six, while others reach eighteen pounds. The difference in weight is probably related to the quantity and quality of food available to the mother during the *gestation period*, or pregnancy. Caribou calves that weigh less than about eight pounds appear to be weak and underdeveloped, and they probably do not live more than a few days.

Caribou calves double their weight in ten to fifteen days, depending upon their size at birth, smaller calves gaining weight more rapidly than the large ones. This rapid growth rate is important, especially in the high north, where the growing

41

A newborn calf struggles to its feet for the first time, while the mother watches for danger.

season for plants is restricted mostly to July. Most caribou calves, however, have about four months of growth before winter arrives.

THE NEWBORN CALF

A caribou cow commences licking and cleaning her calf within a few minutes after its birth. She licks the entire body, and then concentrates on the face. There is frequent contact between the cow and its calf, with the cow licking, nudging, bumping, and touching the calf almost constantly.

Caribou calves are precocious, meaning that they can walk within a short time of birth. In the first half hour after birth

Bent-legged posture of this not-quite-dry caribou calf indicates that it was just born. Legs will straighten as the animal grows older.

most calves stand briefly, but soon lose their balance when they do.

In the second half hour all calves are able to stand. Some move a few yards at a time, but lose balance often. The hind legs are curved inward, pointing toward one another at the hock joints, and they are bent sharply. The feet are placed far apart, and the body sways from side to side.

When a calf is from one to four hours old, it is able to follow its mother at a walk for at least a few yards or even up to a mile, depending upon the individual calf. The hind legs are still sharply bent, and the lower part of the hind leg is carried parallel to the ground. The calf loses balance occasionally, but it seems more certain in placing its feet, and it doesn't sway as much. As it stands or walks, its back appears humped, and the neck dips sharply.

After four to six hours all calves are able to follow their mothers for long distances. A few calves are still slow and travel about as fast as a fast-walking man. The calf holds the lower part of its hind leg more diagonally to the ground and the humped-back appearance is gone or nearly gone.

After six hours, and up to twenty-four hours, calves can run and trot. They can bound when moving fast. The hind legs, however, remain clearly bent.

On their second day of life two out of three calves show al-most completely straightened hind legs, and they can keep up with their running mothers for long distances. They can also swim.

On their third day of life calves show few of the characteristics of the younger calves—the humped back, the awkward gait, the bent hind legs. They are able to run as fast as or faster than their mothers, although they still tire sooner. At this age they are quite graceful.

With caribou herds moving continuously, those calves that can keep up with the herd are most likely to survive.

Calves younger than five days or so have the most difficult time around other animals, for they are still unsteady on their feet. During the sudden stampeding flight of an alarmed band of caribou, such calves are often knocked to the ground and trampled.

Cow-Calf Communication

Especially a cow with a young calf is very alert, and becomes frightened at any unusual sight, sound, or smell. Such a cow immediately bobs its head at the calf, grunts, and even occasion-ally nudges the calf, urging it to follow. She then flees from the

An anxious caribou cow and her calf

area, the calf at her heels. If the calf is very young and cannot follow easily, she returns to it frequently, bobbing her head, urging it to follow her.

When a caribou mother flees danger with her calf, she almost invariably runs straight up a ridge or hill, if one is near. Sometimes a ridge may be rocky and rough, and the calf may slip and slide and repeatedly fall. Nevertheless, mother caribou instincts tell these creatures that there is safety in the heights.

If a threat appears when a calf is minutes old, and it doesn't or cannot respond to head bobbing, the mother will lie a few feet away facing the calf, her muzzle pointing toward the calf. This must be meaningful to the calf, for when the mother does this, the calf renews its efforts to stand or to walk. Sometimes this is the first time in its life that a calf stands or attempts to walk.

Caribou mothers use other ways to communicate with their young calves. When a predator pursues a caribou cow and her calf, the cow immediately starts to run, urging the infant to follow. She will run in front of the calf at about the fastest speed of the calf. Sometimes a cow will run far ahead of the running calf, only to whirl and return to the calf and bob her head toward it. This usually encourages the calf to run faster.

If the calf doesn't keep up its speed and the predator is getting near, the cow may run beside or just behind the calf. She may then hold her neck extended, with her head at the same level as that of her calf. The cow then grunts continually and may nudge the calf. This, too, is a message to the calf to run faster.

Calf Play

When they are about two weeks old caribou calves spend much time gamboling across the countryside like frolicking lambs. A group of calves will chase one another, play follow the leader, and dash about at full speed. They leap over rocks and even caribou mothers that may be quietly lying about ruminating.

At this impetuous age, the calves seem to depend upon their mothers to find them. Occasionally one sees a caribou calf dashing pell-mell across the tundra, anxiously followed by its mother. The calf apparently wants to explore, to run, to play. The mother simply wants to keep track of her calf.

Lost Calves

Caribou mothers become separated from their calves probably more often than any other ungulate species. There are various reasons for this. Within a few days the calf boldly explores the region around its feeding mother. If the calf has wandered very far and the mother is suddenly startled, they may have difficulty in getting together again.

Caribou herds of hundreds to perhaps thousands often travel

A days-old caribou calf snuggles down next to a snowdrift.

together, scattered across many miles of rugged country. Under such conditions, cows and calves become separated easily. Lost or abandoned caribou calves are a common sight on the calving grounds and along the routes of migrating herds.

Older cows usually spend much time searching for their lost calves, but very young caribou cows seldom bother. In young caribou mothers the urge to travel and to follow the herd may be stronger than the instinct to search for a lost calf.

Young calves are most apt to be the ones left behind by a moving band, simply because they cannot keep up. It appears likely that few calves born of very young (yearling) caribou cows survive the first week of life. In one study, 13 percent of the yearling cows in a herd had calves.

Both the snorting and grunting of the cow and the grunting

of the calf help to bring the two together. Cows seem able to recognize their own calves at least partly by sight.

Positive identification of calves seems to depend upon scent. A searching cow smelling a strange calf simply leaves it and continues her search. If a strange calf wanders near a cow with or without a calf, and she is not searching for a calf, the cow often strikes at it viciously with her head or front hooves. If the cow still has hard antlers she may kill or wound the stray calf.

Cows that have lost calves frequently accept another. Occasionally a cow that has lost its calf tries to attract other calves away from their mothers. Two cows vying for possession of a calf sometimes make it difficult for observers to know which is the true mother. Each cow tries to exclude the other by moving between it and the calf.

Lone calves wandering across the tundra are easy marks for predators; many such calves do not survive. In one study in Alaska, 40 out of every 100 caribou calves born in a herd died during the first year of life. Seventy percent of the deaths came between the time of birth and October, or during the first four months.

Most scientists who have studied caribou agree that nearly half of the calves die during their first year, and the figure is sometimes much higher.

7

Caribou Mortality

Life is uncertain for caribou, and few of them live long. A caribou that is more than ten years old is elderly. Scientists have learned this by studying razor-thin cross sections of caribou teeth under a microscope.

The teeth are cut with a special diamond-edged saw, and ultraviolet light is used to examine the sections. The cementum surrounding the tooth root shows as a series of contrasting bright and dull bands, or growth rings, which are counted like the growth rings of a tree.

Even after a caribou survives the first and most hazardous year, it faces an uncertain future. One study in Alaska showed that 14 out of every 100 caribou one year old or older died each year. Hunters killed an average of eight of these. Wolves killed one or two. Accidents, disease, starvation, and other causes accounted for the other four.

Mortality, however, can vary greatly from one year to the next, depending upon weather, food conditions, disease, or the number of predators. Combinations of these factors change, too.

The number of calves that survive the calving season, the number that survive their first year, and the number that survive each year after that determine whether a caribou herd will grow, remain the same size, or decrease in size.

A wolf (foreground) chasing a band of caribou in Arctic Alaska

PREDATORS

Predators can cause serious losses of caribou, and the wolf is the chief natural predator. This 80- to 140-pound member of the dog family has little difficulty in killing a caribou whenever it wishes. It can run down and catch healthy adult caribou in a long chase. It also often catches its prey by surprise, ambush, or stratagem, in which it may drive a caribou to another waiting wolf.

Most caribou killed by wolves are healthy, normal animals. Wolves also catch and kill crippled and sick caribou, which may have a beneficial effect on the caribou herd as a whole. Diseased and crippled animals, however, are scarce in caribou herds, mainly because they do not survive long.

At various times healthy caribou are handicapped, and become easy prey for wolves. Pregnant cows cannot run as fast or as far as cows that are not pregnant. Calves cannot run at their full speed and distance until they are at least a week, perhaps two weeks, old. Old bulls, which have stored large amounts of fat on their bodies in the fall before breeding season, become winded easily and are often prey to wolves.

When wolves are abundant on caribou calving grounds, they can seriously damage a calf crop. In one year, wolves killed at least one out of every ten newborn calves in one Alaskan herd.

Red fox. Occasionally this little member of the dog family kills caribou calves for food.

When wolves become too numerous and kill too many caribou, they endanger themselves, for often caribou is their main food.

Caribou calves are also vulnerable to attacks from wolverine, coyote, lynx, red fox, eagle, and bear. All of these animals can catch and kill an hours-old, or even a days-old calf.

Both golden and bald eagles may attack calves, kill them, and eat them. Caribou mothers protect their calf from eagle attacks by rearing up and striking at the eagle as it swoops toward the calf. Or they may stand with their calf under their belly until

Bald eagle. This large member of the hawk family occasionally preys on caribou calves.

the eagle leaves.

The raven, which is commonly found on all caribou ranges in Alaska and Canada, occasionally attacks caribou calves. This big, heavy-beaked cousin to the crow speedily plucks out a caribou calf's eyes; the calf then threshes and flounders about until it dies, at which time the raven feeds.

ACCIDENTS

The constant travels of caribou expose the animals to many hazards. The animals break through thin ice and drown. In Canada many have been swept to their death over rapids or waterfalls while swimming swift rivers. Calves frequently drown when their mothers lead them into cold, swift, and wide rivers

Separated from its mother when crossing a swift stream, this calf was rescued by refuge manager, Don Frickie. The calf soon rejoined its mother.

before they are strong enough to swim them properly.

A sudden spring blizzard, occurring during calving, may kill many calves. In June, 1947, such a blizzard killed 80 percent of the calves in one area of the Canadian Arctic.

Snowslides, rockslides, falls from steep cliffs, becoming entangled with wire or rope carelessly left by man, broken legs from traveling on rocky ground—all may either kill or cripple a caribou. A crippled caribou cannot easily escape predators, and it may not even be able to travel enough to obtain the food it needs. A caribou with an injured front foot will almost surely die in winter, for then it cannot dig through the snow for the food it needs.

INSECT PESTS

Flies and mosquitoes are sometimes serious pests to caribou, and occasionally have even caused death. These persistent pests attack where the fur is thin; ears that are bitten become swollen, and the eyes and lips are ringed with hundreds of clinging mosquitoes and black flies.

The warble fly and the nostril fly, or nose-bot, are two parasitic pests of caribou. The warble fly is a large, orange and black, beelike fly. Almost all caribou are infested with it. The adult is on the wing about three weeks during July and August, although in favorable years it may be active for about three months. This fly makes a low buzz in flight and darts about rapidly, often landing on rocks. The adult form lives from four to nine days. As an adult, this fly deposits its eggs on the hair of caribou. The larvae hatch, bore through the skin, and migrate to the back region where they remain to develop just under the skin. Here they live through the winter, until in June they emerge through a hole they have eaten in the skin, and drop to the ground. The skin area along the back of almost all caribou is scarred from the holes made by these grubs. The grubs then develop into pupae, and in 16 to 31 days the adult flies emerge, and the cycle commences again as the adults lay eggs on the hair of caribou.

The nose-bot fly is a large, black, beelike insect with a round abdomen. Adults are on the wing during the same time as the warble fly. Although it isn't as plentiful as the warble fly, the nose-bot apparently is far more annoying to caribou. Fifty percent of the Arctic caribou herd in Alaska was found to have nose-bot larvae, as was 80 percent of the Nelchina herd.

Eggs of the nose-bot hatch in the adult fly. The tiny larvae that result are deposited by the fly in the nostrils of the caribou. The initial growth of the larvae probably takes place in the nose and head sinuses of the caribou. Eventually the larvae attach in small clusters inside the throat.

There may be from a few to as many as 200, with an average of 50, of these tiny larvae attached to the inside of the throat of a single caribou.

The larvae which mature in May are an inch or more long. They detach from the throat and apparently irritate the caribou, which sneezes, snorts, and coughs, as the larvae leave and fall to the ground.

Pupation takes place generally in five or six hours, and the pupal stage lasts from 16 to 56 days, depending upon temperature. Adult flies emerge during June and July, and live for 10 to 13 days. The cycle is then repeated, with the larvae spending until the following May in the throat of the host caribou.

Although caribou are terrified of warble and nose-bot flies and may run wildly to try to escape them, neither is thought to cause any direct mortality. However they may contribute to overall poor condition of caribou, which may in the end lead to mortality.

8

Caribou and Man

The caribou has made man's existence possible in regions where otherwise it would have been hard or impossible for him to survive. It has the place in the North of domestic livestock in more settled or farming areas, and is to the northern Indian and Eskimo what the bison was to the plains Indians.

The caribou has been the cornerstone of life for some Eskimo and Athabascan Indians, and the cultures of some areas have been based entirely upon caribou. The Chipewyans, one of the branches of the Athabascan Indians living on the northern edge of the Canadian woods, gained the name of "caribou-eaters."

Indians and Eskimos in other areas of the North still depend heavily upon caribou, using not only the meat and hide, but other parts of the animal as well. Sewing thread is made from the sinew found along the backbone. To protect the eyes from the sun's glare on snow, snow goggles with tiny slits are made from the smooth and shiny hooves. In the distant past, tools were made from caribou antlers.

CARIBOU MEAT

Caribou meat has a mild flavor and is highly nutritious. Favorite cuts are found on the rump, and the tongue and the marrow in the leg bones are considered to be delicacies. Tips of antlers in velvet are also sometimes eaten. *Akútuk*, an Eskimo

55

The Eskimo village of Anaktuvuk Pass, high in the Brooks Range of Arctic Alaska. About 125 Eskimos live here and depend almost entirely upon caribou for food.

dish, is whipped caribou fat. Sometimes berries are added, at other times dried meat or fish is mixed in.

Cuts of meat are usually boiled by Eskimos and Indians, although sometimes they are fried. They may be preserved by being cut into long, thin strips and hung over poles to dry. Dry meat may last for months, and it can be eaten dry, or it may be boiled.

During the cold months, from September through May, caribou meat can be left outside and be preserved by the cold. Frozen meat may be chopped off and eaten without cooking, or pieces may be chopped with an axe and boiled.

Food found in the stomach of freshly killed caribou is sometimes eaten by Eskimos. It provides valuable vitamins needed in winter, when most plants that are eaten by humans are buried beneath snow. Back fat, which may be two or three inches thick in the fall and weigh twenty to thirty pounds on old bulls, is valuable and is added to lean meat to provide energy food.

For centuries, caribou meat was used to feed sled dogs, and it

Eskimo boys on a cache that holds the winter supply of caribou meat for their family

is still important where dogs are kept, and where caribou are abundant. A team of six sled dogs eats about fifty caribou a year.

CARIBOU SKIN

No clothing is warmer than that made from caribou skins. Hides taken from calf and yearling caribou shot in August and September are best for clothing, for they are softer, more flexible, and with shorter, finer fur. Modern clothing, often insulated with waterfowl down, has replaced certain parts of the clothing of northerners. However, when the warmest possible clothing is desired, caribou skins are used.

A complete Eskimo winter caribou-skin outfit consists of an inner and outer suit. The inner suit is worn with the fur side in, and is generally made of the softest and finest of skins. The outer suit, which includes the hooded parka and pants, is used with the hair side out. Winter boots are made from the thin skin of caribou legs. Formerly, when no other skins were available, boot soles were made from the thick neck skin of old bull caribou.

After September caribou hair grows so long and thick that the hides are no longer suitable for clothing. They are then used in making sleeping robes, beds, for covering doors and roofs for added insulation, and for use as robes in sleds.

Skins of caribou may also be cleaned of hair and used to cover kayaks. Strips of hide are used to tie the sled parts together, for making webbing for snowshoes, and for all of the many uses of rope and string. The rawhide can be soaked in water and tied tightly; as it dries, it shrinks, tightening the binding and becoming exceedingly hard.

At one time, an important use of winter caribou hides was for making tents. When canvas became available to the Eskimos and

Simon Paneak, an Eskimo of Anaktuvuk Pass, with a caribou-skin kayak he has constructed.

Alaskan Eskimos returning home with caribou. Snow machines have re-placed dog teams in much of Alaska.

Indians, it was often used on top of the caribou hides, to keep the hides from getting wet. Today it is rare to find an Eskimo or Indian using a caribou skin tent. Twenty or more hides are needed to make the usual caribou skin tent.

HUNTING CARIBOU

Before they had rifles, some of Alaska's Indians made pole fences, sometimes several miles long, across the path of migrating caribou. Gaps were left in the fence here and there, and in the gaps, rawhide nooses were set, which snared the animals as they passed through.

Eskimos occasionally build a "caribou fence" with a long line of low sod or rock piles, built to resemble men. Hunters leap into sight near the piles. The caribou see the long line of the devices, think they are men, and flee to where the Eskimos want them—to waiting hunters.

Eskimo, Indian, and white hunters harvest perhaps 30,000 caribou a year in Alaska. Wildlife biologists, working for the state of Alaska, continually study the herds, counting them from airplanes, recording the number of calves born each year, and keeping track of increases or decreases of the herds.

In Canada, between 1920 and 1950, from 100,000 to 200,000 caribou a year were killed by humans. The kill today is far less, as Eskimos and Indians have gradually left their original life style.

If a herd starts to decrease, hunting may be reduced by setting smaller bag limits or shorter seasons. If that isn't effective, hunting may be stopped until that herd again increases. On the other

Calf number 258 lying flat on the tundra. The metal tag in its ear will provide scientists with information about caribou migrations.

hand, if no hunting occurs, caribou herds have a tendency to increase until there are too many animals for the available winter food. When this happens the herds migrate farther and farther, searching for food. With a shortage of food, the condition of the animals becomes poor, and they become easy prey for predators, starvation, and disease. A herd that grows too large may "crash" with large numbers dying.

All caribou herds seem to follow this boom and bust cycle. In the 1930s, for example, Alaska had an estimated 1,000,000 caribou. By the 1950s there were probably fewer than 200,000 in the Territory.

Alaska's Nelchina herd numbered about 10,000 in 1945. By 1962 it had increased to about 71,000. In 1972 it was back down to about 10,000 animals.

When caribou are properly managed, the animals harvested by man are above and beyond those needed to maintain a healthy herd size. Farmers use the same principal in managing cattle, chickens, pigs, sheep, and other living resources that are important as food.

CARIBOU HABITAT

Range conditions and weather probably have a greater influence on caribou numbers than man has up to now.

However, as man continues to settle northern regions, the range of the caribou as well as its numbers will continue to decline. Caribou require vast, wide open areas to roam in. Pipelines for oil and gas, highways, railroads, power lines, new towns, villages, wilderness resorts, airports—all gradually will change the natural home of the caribou, diverting the animals from their natural movements. The 789-mile trans-Alaska hot oil pipeline from the Arctic Ocean to the Gulf of Alaska, scheduled for completion in summer 1977, cuts in half a great region north of the Yukon River that previously had no roads, and no pipelines. This pipeline and a paralleling road are probably the first of many, for Arctic Alaska and Canada both apparently have great untapped oil reserves.

While some sections of the Trans-Alaska pipeline were to be buried (about half in preliminary estimates), sections where there is permafrost cannot be buried, for the hot pipeline would melt the frozen soil, sag, and probably break. Instead, sections of the pipeline being built in permafrost areas are being constructed above ground. Since the pipeline is four feet in diameter and is elevated four feet off the ground when it isn't buried, this presents a large barrier to migrating caribou.

Caribou probably would not freely cross large, above-ground pipes. During one study in Alaska, scientists watched as wild caribou approached a simulated pipeline. Only 994 out of 5,599 (17.6 percent) crossed over the two gravel ramps built over the six- to eight-foot barrier. Fewer than 5 percent used four underpasses built into the structure, and a smaller number crawled under the simulated pipeline. The rest of the caribou went around the 7,100-foot-long barrier (42.4 percent of the animals) or turned back when they were confronted with the obstacle (34.4 percent).

In Norway, wild reindeer have been obstructed from their natural movements by highways and railroads. One herd abandoned its traditional wintering grounds because of this. Alaska's caribou experts think that the days of herds of hundreds of thousands of caribou in nothern Alaska are probably a thing of the past because of the expected impact of highways and pipelines, and other human activities. Animals driven from their chosen range cannot always be expected to find good habitat elsewhere, and their chances of survival will likely be lessened.

Selected Bibliography

Banfield, A.W.F., 1951, *The Barren-Ground Caribou*. Canadian Wildlife Service, Department of Resources Development, Ottawa, 56 pp. Good early report on Canada's caribou.

Crisler, L., 1958, *Arctic Wild*. Harper and Brothers, New York. 301 pp. Good popular account of caribou land, caribou, and wolves.

Kelsall, J.P., 1968, *The Migratory Barren-Ground Caribou of Canada*. Canadian Wildlife Service, Monograph No. 3. Queen's Printer, Ottawa. Best reference on Canada's caribou.

Leopold, A.S., and Darling, F.F., 1953, *Wildlife in Alaska*. Ronald Press Company, New York. 129 pp. Accurate report on history of Alaska's important wildlife.

Murie, Adolph, 1944, *The Wolves of Mount McKinley*. U.S. National Park Service, Fauna National Parks, U.S. Fauna Series, 238 pp. A classic study of the relationship between wolves and various other animals, including caribou.

Murie, O.J., 1935, *Alaska-Yukon Caribou*. U.S. Bureau of Biological Survey, North American Fauna, 93 pp. A classic early study of caribou, with much interesting history.

Pruitt, W.O., Jr., 1966, *Animals of the North*. Harper and Row, New York. General background on many northern species, including caribou.

Rearden, Jim, 1974, Caribou: Hardy Nomads of the North. *National Geographic* magazine, vol. 146, no. 6, (Dec.), pp. 858–878, 17 color photos. A popular account of Alaska's caribou and its status.

Index

DATE			
Mo. Benson			
APR 3 '97			
MAR 1 " 2010			
APR 2 6 2010			

599
RE
Rearden, Jim
Wonders of caribou